GW00694583

This edition copyright
© 2000 Lion Publishing
Illustrations copyright
© 2000 Katarzyna Klein
Published by
Lion Publishing plc
Sandy Lane West, Oxford,
England
www.lion-publishing.co.uk
ISBN 0 7459 4176 1
First edition 2000
10 9 8 7 6 5 4 3 2 1 0

Acknowledgments
pp. 17, 30, 31, 34, 52, 58:
Psalm 30:5, Psalm 46:1–2,
Matthew 28:20, Isaiah 40:31,
Psalm 126:6, Song of Songs
2:11–12, from The New
Revised Standard Version
of the Bible, Anglicized
Edition, copyright © 1989,
1995 by the Division of
Christian Education of the
National Council of the
Churches of Christ in the
United States of America,
and used by permission.

p. 25: from The Prayer Tree,
published Lion Publishing,
copyright © 1991 Michael
Leunig.

p. 28: from A Common Prayer,
published Lion Publishing,
copyright © 1990 and 1997
Michael Leunig.

p. 54: from To You the Living:
Poems of Bereavement and Loss
by Marjorie Pizer, Pinchgut
Press, 6 Oaks Avenue,
Cremorne, Sydney, Australia,
2090. Used by permission.

p. 61: from 'Eurydice' in
Collected Poems by Edith
Sitwell, published Macmillan
1957. Used by permission of
David Higham Associates.

A catalogue record for this
book is available from the
British Library

Typeset in Nueva Roman
Printed and bound in
Singapore

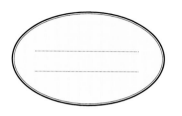

Words of
COMFORT

Compiled by Meryl Doney

LION
Giftlines

CONTENTS

INTRODUCTION

*T*he most beautiful words, those that give the most genuine help, are often born in a silence filled with suffering.

LADISLAUS BOROS

Sometimes it helps to realize that we are not alone in our troubles. Comfort is often to be found in the words of others who have felt the same things and wrestled with the same fears. The thoughts and insights in this collection express a deep sense of purpose: that our experiences are not meaningless, but will ultimately help us to grow and to offer, in our turn, comfort and hope to others.

Words of
COMFORT

A moment's insight is sometimes worth a life's experience.

OLIVER WENDELL HOLMES SR

*O*ne who has journeyed

in a strange land

cannot return unchanged.

C.S. LEWIS

I don't envy those who have never known any pain, physical or spiritual, because I strongly suspect that the capacity for pain and the capacity for joy are equal. Only those who have suffered great pain are able to know equally great joy.

MADELEINE L'ENGLE

*W*eeping may linger for the night,

but joy comes with the morning.

FROM THE OLD TESTAMENT
BOOK OF PSALMS

Without winter,
there can be no spring.
Without mistakes,
there can be no learning.
Without doubts,
there can be no faith.
Without fears,
there can be no courage.

My mistakes, my fears and my doubts are my path to wisdom, faith and courage.

AUTHOR UNKNOWN

A fallen soufflé is just a risen omelette. It depends on how you look at it, that's all – from above or below.

RABBI LIONEL BLUE

Help in
TROUBLE

The darkness of night,
like pain, is dumb.
The darkness of dawn,
like peace, is silent.

RABINDRANATH TAGORE

I cannot hold thee fast,

though thou art mine:

Hold thou me fast,

So earth shall know at last

and heaven at last

That I am thine.

CHRISTINA ROSSETTI

To weep is to make less
the depth of grief.

WILLIAM SHAKESPEARE

$\mathcal{G}$od help us

If our world should grow dark;

And there is no way of seeing

  or knowing.

Grant us courage and trust

To touch and be touched

To find our way onwards

By feeling.

MICHAEL LEUNIG

Give sorrow words:
the grief that does not speak
Whispers the o'er fraught heart,
and bids it break.

WILLIAM SHAKESPEARE

*H*old thou my hands!

In grief and joy, in hope and fear,

Lord, let me feel that thou art near:

Hold thou my hands!

WILLIAM CANTON

God give us strength.
Strength to hold on
and strength to let go.

Michael Leunig

Springs of
COMFORT

God is our refuge and strength:

a very present help in trouble.

Therefore we will not fear,

though the earth should change,

though the mountains shake

in the heart of the sea.

FROM THE OLD TESTAMENT
BOOK OF PSALMS

*J*esus said: 'I am with you always, to the end of the age.'

FROM THE NEW TESTAMENT
GOSPEL OF MATTHEW

All my hurts

My garden spade can heal.

A woodland walk,

A quest of river grapes,

a mocking thrush,

A wild rose,

a rock-loving columbine,

Salve my worst wounds.

RALPH WALDO EMERSON

To read, to think, to love, to hope, to pray – these are the things that make us happy.

JOHN RUSKIN

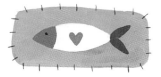

*T*hose who wait for the Lord

shall renew their strength,

they shall mount up with wings

   like eagles,

they shall run and not be weary,

they shall walk and not faint.

From the Old Testament
book of Isaiah

Whether I fly with angels,

    fall with dust,

Thy hands made both,

    and I am there:

Thy power and love,

    my love and trust

Make one place everywhere.

GEORGE HERBERT

Let nothing disturb you;

Let nothing dismay you;

All things pass,

God never changes.

St Teresa of Avila

Finding a
PATTERN

Conquer by accepting. Pain, like other elemental forces in nature, can be turned to use, but only if the laws of its operation are first understood and conformed to.

Those who meet it clear-eyed and with a positive and active acceptance make a strange discovery. They find that they achieve an enrichment and a growth of personality which makes them centres of influence and light.

BURNET HILLMAN STREETER

But is there for the night

   a resting-place?

'A roof for when the slow

   dark hours begin.'

May not the darkness

   hide it from my face?

'You cannot miss that inn.'

Shall I find comfort,
   travel-sore and weak?
'Of labour you shall find the sum.'
Will there be beds for me
   and all who seek?
'Yea, beds for all who come.'

CHRISTINA ROSSETTI

*T*he dark threads are as needful

In the weaver's skilful hand

As the threads of gold and silver

In the pattern he has planned.

AUTHOR UNKNOWN

*T*o yield is to be preserved whole.

To be bent is to become straight.

To be empty is to be full.

To be worn out is to be renewed.

LAO TSU

People may perform astonishing feats and comprehend a vast amount of knowledge and yet have no understanding of themselves. But suffering directs them to look within.

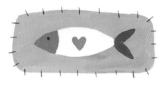

If it succeeds, then there, within them, is the beginning of their learning.

SØREN KIERKEGAARD

A deep distress

has humanized my soul.

WILLIAM WORDSWORTH

*W*hither away delight?

Thou cam'st but now; wilt thou

   so soon depart,

And give me up to night?

For many weeks of lingering

   pain and smart

But one half hour of comfort

   for my heart?

<small>GEORGE HERBERT</small>

Man was made for joy and woe;
And when this we rightly know
Through the world we safely go.
Joy and woe are woven fine.
A clothing for the soul divine;
Under every grief and pine
Runs a joy with silken twine.

WILLIAM BLAKE

$\mathcal{G}$od's promise of resurrection
is written not only in books
but in every springtime leaf.

MARTIN LUTHER

*O*ften the test of courage

is not to die but to live.

VITTORIO ALFIERI

Comfort and
JOY

Those who go out weeping,

bearing the seed for sowing,

shall come home

 with shouts of joy,

carrying their sheaves.

FROM THE OLD TESTAMENT
BOOK OF PSALMS

*G*rief is itself a medicine.

WILLIAM COWPER

I am emerging
  from an ocean of grief…
I am seeing the living
  that is to be lived,
The laughter
  that is to be laughed,
The joy
  that is to be enjoyed,

The loving

  that is to be accomplished.

I am learning at last

The tremendous triumph of life.

MARJORIE PIZER

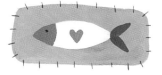

And time remembered
is grief forgotten,
And frosts are slain
and flowers begotten,
And in green underwood
and cover
Blossom by blossom
the spring begins.

ALGERNON CHARLES SWINBURNE

If Winter comes,

can Spring be far behind?

PERCY BYSSHE SHELLEY

For now the winter is past,

the rain is over and gone.

The flowers appear on the earth;

the time of singing has come,

and the voice of the turtle-dove

is heard in our land.

FROM THE OLD TESTAMENT
SONG OF SONGS

In the midst of winter
I found at last there
was within myself
an invincible summer.

ALBERT CAMUS

Thou that hast given
  so much to me,
Give one thing more,
  a grateful heart.
Not thankful when it pleases me,
As if thy blessings had spare days;
But such a heart
  whose very pulse may be
Thy praise.

GEORGE HERBERT

Love is not changed by death,
And nothing is lost
and all in the end is harvest.

EDITH SITWELL